West Yorkshire Stations

on old picture postcards

Norman Ellis

1. Bradford Forster Square station in LMS days. Replacing an earlier station, it was built in 1890 and known as Market Street station until 1924. To the left of the arcaded facade is the Midland Hotel; to its right the front of Valley Road goods depot. Airedale, Wharfedale, Morecambe, Leeds and London were some of the places linked to Forster Square station. Today, it has lost its overall roof and sees much less traffic than formerly.

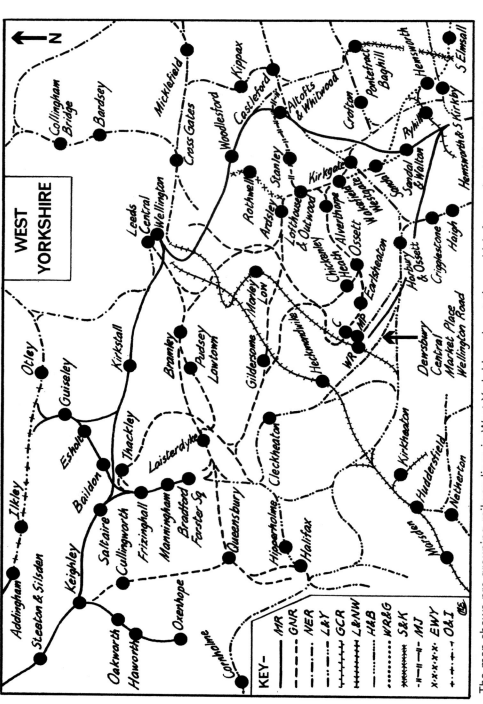

The map shows pre-grouping railway lines in West Yorkshire, plus stations which feature in the book. It is not to scale. Some less important or mainly freight lines have been omitted.

WEST YORKSHIRE

KEY-
MR
GNR
NER
L&Y
GCR
L&NW
H&B
WR&G
S&K
MJ
EWY
O&I

MANNINGHAM STATION

2. One mile north of Forster Square was **Manningham** station, shown here c. 1907 with a train for Bradford. The suburb grew after the opening of the large Manningham Mills. Crowds used to arrive by train from a wide area for the big galas held in nearby Peel Park. The station, which opened in 1868, was closed to passengers in 1965 and goods in 1968.

Introduction

Early in 2001, Leeds railway station became famous for its lack of trains. The roads surrounding the ghost station were at times crammed with so many buses and coaches that the complex seemed to be turning into a coach terminal. The road vehicles had been requisitioned to ferry people to various other stations, including York, Bradford and Wakefield. London trains, which normally started from Leeds, were starting and finishing their journeys at Wakefield.

Crucially, Leeds station, which had suffered increasingly from congestion, was being upgraded. The work had been proceeding for months. Essential track and signalling work, much of which was due for completion over the Christmas and New Year period, fell behind schedule. On 2nd January, would-be-travellers, some of them eager to begin work after the long holiday, arrived late at their destinations, if at all. It wasn't leaves on the line. Two falls of snow and sub-zero temperatures over the holiday period were partly to blame. Railtrack and the various train operating companies which run into Leeds may eventually live this one down. Suddenly you recognize the importance of the railway system.

The City of Leeds is in the Metropolitan County of West Yorkshire, which was created from part of the time-honoured West Riding in 1974. The carve-up separated the textile-based regions of the north from the steel-based regions further south, which became South Yorkshire. These traditional industries, along with coalmining, have suffered from decline. The County of West Yorkshire consists of the Metropolitan Districts of Bradford, Leeds, Wakefield, Calderdale (including Halifax) and Kirklees (including Huddersfield and Dewsbury). In the latter half of the 19th century, this largely industrialised section of the West Riding attracted various railway companies, who were eager to secure a share of passenger and goods traffic.

During the formation of the country's railway system, rivalry difficulties were overcome and great constructional feats achieved. Railways reached a peak in the Edwardian era, by which time many railway companies had been amalgamated to form larger organisations. Six of these became established in West Yorkshire. These were the Midland Railway, Lancashire & Yorkshire Railway, London & North Western Railway, North Eastern Railway, Great Northern Railway and (to a lesser extent) Great Central Railway. Following the grouping of railways in 1923, the first three became part of the London, Midland & Scottish Railway, whilst the remainder formed part of the London & North Eastern Railway.

The railways were nationalised in 1947. Postwar modernisation included the phasing out of steam and implementation of the Beeching Plan. The latter was responsible for a drastic reduction in the size of the country's rail system. The network in West Yorkshire, although still comprehensive, has been much diluted. Some new stations have been opened and passengers won back.

Decades ago, before locomotives and trains were being snapped by railway buffs, a different breed of photographer was purposefully taking pictures of stations. The images fitted into the same category as churches, town halls and streets. They were printed on to a piece of material with the word 'postcard' on the reverse, either to be mailed, stored in an album, or both. The railway stations were, like streets or churches, part of a way of life. The old station buildings have largely disappeared. This book is a testimony to the stations and those who recorded them.

Most of the pictures are reproduced from postcards in the author's collection; a few cards were kindly loaned by Brian Lund.

Norman Ellis
July 2001

3. North from Manningham, the next station was **Frizinghall**, seen here c.1907. Its stocky main building, left, contrasts with the waiting shelter opposite, with its curved roof. Opening in 1875, the station was closed in 1965, but was reopened in simplified form in 1987.

4. Titus Salt founded the village of Saltaire around his mohair and alpaca factory. **Saltaire** station, pictured c.1930 on a card by Walter Scott of Bradford, was nearest for Shipley Glen and its tramway. The station, which originated in 1859, was closed in 1965, but rebuilt and reopened in 1984.

An archetypal Village Station

In September 1939, the *London & North Eastern Railway Magazine* published an article written by Mr S. Cook, stationmaster at Lofthouse & Outwood station *(see illustration 21)*. The following extracts are taken from it. They remind us that even the smaller stations were involved with both passenger and freight operations and that working there was almost a way of life.

Situated 6 miles from Leeds and 3 miles from Wakefield, passengers travelling from Leeds to London may, when approaching Lofthouse, observe the headgear of Lofthouse Colliery on the left. The unsightly pit heap is much in evidence, particularly when the waste products are burning. The village of Outwood lies on the east side of the station and Lofthouse village about two miles towards Leeds.

Near the station may be seen acres of rhubarb fields. This produce is allowed to grow without interference for two or three years, then the rhubarb roots are gathered and planted in sheds. About November, the sheds are heated, principally with coke. No light must be visible, otherwise the beautiful pale strawberry-coloured sticks of rhubarb would not be possible in December. This traffic is usually at its best from December to March. This season, no less than 272 wagons, with a tonnage of 520, were dispatched to London, Manchester, Sheffield, etc. The traffic is forwarded by express goods service for early morning markets.

A favourite hobby in which the miner indulges is pigeon racing. During the summer season, large quantities of pigeons may be seen on the platform awaiting despatch. It is characteristic of each consignee to put his own consignment into the guard's brake, so concerned is he for the welfare of his birds.

This station has a reputation to maintain in connection with St. John Ambulance. During the greater part of the year, a team of a dozen to twenty meet together every Sunday morning and go through various drills. The team has competed in the district ambulance competitions every year since its inception. They have won five trophies, and one day they hope to bring the shield from London.

Some mention must be made respecting the distinction which Lofthouse station holds for its gardens and general layout. Nine first class and two second class prizes have been awarded. It will be appreciated that, being adjacent to a colliery, a good garden display and cleanliness of the premises are difficult to maintain. The three passenger porters are determined to keep up the standard of the past nine years, and one day the staff hope to receive the much-coveted 'special' prize. The station generally is one that creates much public interest, not only amongst the passengers joining and alighting, but also the local inhabitants, who may be seen standing on the railway bridge situated on the public highway, watching its progress.

5. Keighley station, c.1911. It was built in 1883 to replace an earlier station on the opposite side of Bradford Road. The platform shown here is still used by trains between Bradford and Skipton. The evocative scene can now be recaptured by moving to another platform and watching Worth Valley steam trains leave for Oxenhope.

6. Opening in 1892, **Steeton & Silsden** station replaced an earlier one on a different site. The view, looking towards Keighley c.1911, shows a typical Midland Railway building with three gabled pavilions, although two was more usual. The station closed in 1965, but was rebuilt and reopened in 1990 at a cost of £260,000.

7. The MR branch to Oxenhope was opened in 1867, partly to serve the valley's textile mills. After closure in 1962, it was reopened by the Keighley & Worth Valley Railway Preservation Society in 1968. The view of **Oakworth** station dates from 1913. The left-hand building is an addition in a different style. Note the barrow, clock and postbox.

8. Stripped of much of its industry, the Worth Valley is now a tourist area with excellent walks and much of interest to Bronte devotees. This busy scene, c.1905, shows **Haworth** station against a background of houses and mills. The people on the station are dressed in their finery.

9. This card of **Oxenhope** station shows the building's different architectural styles. It was posted from the village in March 1907 with the message, *"This is where I am spending my Easter holidays."* The 10-ton capacity crane indicates the presence of a large goods yard behind the station.

10. Trains from Bradford reached Ilkley via Guiseley. The first station beyond Shipley junction was **Baildon,** opened in 1876 and shown here c.1910. In the far distance are coal sidings, a goods shed and signal box. Baildon station was twice closed (1953 and 1957) but was reopened in 1977 with only basic facilities.

11. When the MR opened **Esholt** station in 1876, it opted for straightforward timber buildings, because the passenger potential was not great. The station, pictured here c. 1910 with an Ilkley-Bradford train approaching, was closed in 1940, although the buildings remained until 1953.

12. Guiseley station, which opened in 1865, was provided with a sturdy stone building on its down platform. Visible next to it is a feeder tank for water columns at the ends of the platforms. The postcard was published by C. & A.G. Lewis, Nottingham, c.1922. The old stone buildings were replaced by modest stone structures in 1974.

13. The MR constructed a line from Ilkley to Skipton via Addingham in 1888. The main station building at **Addingham,** photographed c.1913, is a smaller form of that at Steeton (*see illus 6*). Beyond the platforms, a signal cabin and goods shed are visible. The station closed in 1965.

14. Kirkstall station was on the Shipley-Leeds line, which opened in 1846. During route widening in 1905, Kirkstall received a new station, depicted here when nearing completion. The card, sold by G. & J. Richardson, printers, Kirkstall, was posted from there on 12th August 1905. Closure came in 1965.

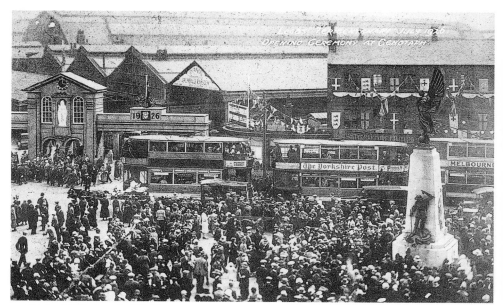

15. In 1926, **Leeds Wellington** station received a temporary facade for the city's tercentenary celebrations, held from 8th-17th July. Centrepiece was a replica of the front of the Moot Hall, which once stood in Briggate. The card depicts the first day, with the facade to the left and the station beyond.

16. Woodlesford station, opened in 1840, dates from North Midland (later MR) days. Staggered platforms and a house-shaped main building are featured here. The station, minus its old buildings, is still open. The card, from E.J. Bloor, photo publisher, Castleford, was posted from Leeds to Pontefract on 18th October 1906.

17. Mining subsidence may have influenced the MR in its choice of timber platforms and buildings at **Altofts & Whitwood** station, shown here in LMS days, c.1925. The station, which opened in 1870, was midway between the two villages. After becoming run down, it was closed in 1990.

18. Opened in 1870, **Sandal & Walton** station was much nearer Walton than Sandal. Here, c.1905, the stationmaster and some of his staff pose in front of the Tudor-style stone building, whose design is redolent of the somewhat elitist area. The station was closed in 1961.

19. Although jointly owned, **Leeds Central** station was always associated with the GNR. Built in 1848-57, it lacked architectural merit but, after the 1923 grouping, saw the introduction of various prestige Pullman trains. Probably the lads in this Edwardian staff group at Central are messenger boys. Closure came in 1967.

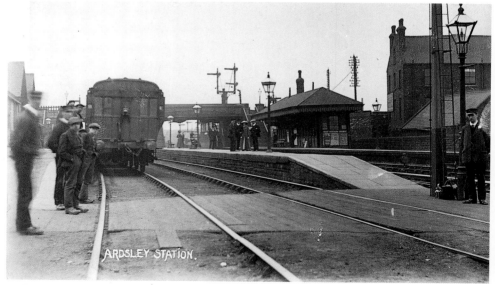

20. A line from Leeds Central ran south through Ardsley to Wakefield and beyond. With a colliery, ironworks, brickworks, mills and GNR engine sheds nearby, **Ardsley** station was frequently covered in a pall of smoke. Some of its five platforms are shown, c.1907. The station was opened in 1857 and closed to passengers in 1964.

21. The main building at **Lofthouse & Outwood** station is pictured c.1906. The timber and glass structure includes a booking hall, waiting rooms and toilets. The station was opened in 1858, closed in 1960, but reopened on the opposite side of the road in 1988. Through the bridge on the right are the platforms of the Methley Joint Railway.

22. Replacing another one nearby, **Wakefield Westgate** station was opened for the GNR and two other companies in 1867. Looking north, the view shows the station's ridge-and-furrow canopies, c.1911, on a card by H.M. Wilson, photographer, 28 Wood Street, Wakefield. The station has been much altered over the years.

ALVERTHORPE STN.

23. Alverthorpe station was on a branch from Wrenthorpe Junction to Dewsbury. The station is pictured on a card by E.I. Walker, who preceded Wilson at the Wood Street premises. It was posted from Wakefield to Ilkley in 1904. The track fanned into two sidings beyond the gate. Built in 1872, the station lasted until 1954.

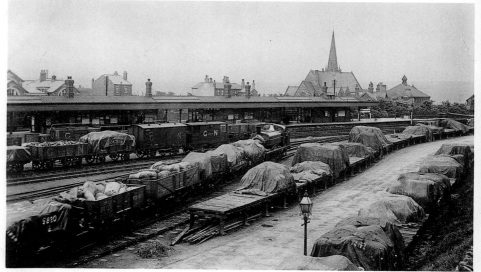

OSSETT STATION.

24. The first **Ossett** station, dating from 1864, was replaced by this one in 1889. The thriving mungo and shoddy trade demanded a large station and goods yard. The view, looking towards the Green, was produced for W.C. Machan, Wakefield, c.1910. After closure in 1964, houses were built on the site.

25. Earlsheaton station was opened in 1875. A timetable for July 1906, the approximate date of the photo, shows that sixty passenger trains stopped every weekday, with twelve on Sundays. In the 1930s, club trips to Bridlington and Cleethorpes became popular. A cattle dock and private sidings adjoined the station. Passenger services were withdrawn in 1953; other facilities in 1963.

26. Dewsbury Central station was the oldest of three in the town. It provided a link with Bradford, Leeds and Wakefield. Pictured c.1905, the island platform has a long building with ride-and-furrow canopies at both sides. Access from street level was via a flight of steps. Opened in 1848, the station closed 90 years later.

27. Chickenley Heath was the only intermediate passenger station on the GNR direct branch from Ossett to Batley. The station opened in 1877, and is seen with one of the company's innovative steam rail motors, shortly before closure to passengers in 1909 as a result of tram competition. Mineral traffic continued along the line for a period.

28. The GNR's **Gildersome** station was opened in 1856 and photographed c.1905. The double-gabled station house sits uncomfortably amongst the plainer buildings, which provide space for posters. Passenger and goods services ended in 1955 and 1965 respectively. Gildersome's L&NW station only lasted from 1900 to 1921.

BRAMLEY STATION.

RELIABLE [WR] SERIES 765 / 26

29. Today, **Bramley** station, which opened in 1854, is little more than two platforms with small shelters, having been reopened in 1983 after closure in 1966. On this c.1910 view, the main station building towers in the background. To the right is the large goods yard, with coal depots. 'Reliable' series card no. 765.26 by William Ritchie, Edinburgh.

Lowtown Station, Pudsey.

30. A half dozen people await arrival of a westbound train a**t Pudsey Lowtown** station, c.1908. The geometric embellishments on the canopy ends appeared also at Pudsey's other GNR station, called Greenside. Protective end screens were a feature of many GNR canopies. Both stations were opened in 1878 and closed in 1964.

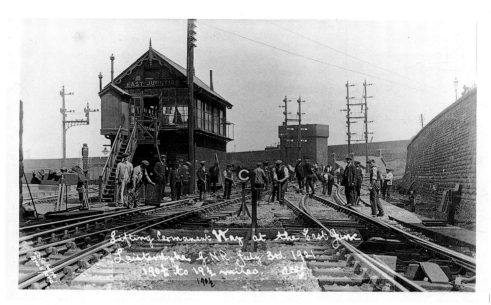

31. Men at work! Lifting permanent way on Sunday 3rd July 1921 at East Junction, Laisterdyke, 700 yards from **Laisterdyke** station. This was one of five busy GNR junctions to the east and south of the station. Postcard by Coldham of Bradford.

32. The Laisterdyke-Shipley branch, with three intermediate stations, was inaugurated in 1874. Traffic included limestone from Ingleton and Skipton for ironworks around Low Moor. Passenger business was less successful and withdrawn in 1931, when the branch's **Thackley** station, above, was closed. Track was singled and used for freight until the 1960s.

33. GNR lines radiating from Queensbury were heavily engineered, with viaducts, tunnels and severe gradients. **Queensbury** station was constructed in 1879, with double platforms on each side of a triangular junction. Platform buildings were added a decade later. The platform for Keighley to Bradford trains is on the right of this c.1905 view. Regular passenger services ceased in

34. *"I thought I would send you a PC of the old place."* The card of **Cullingworth** station was posted from Keighley c.1915. Until the 1939-45 War, the station, shown looking towards Keighley, boasted plenty of goods and passenger traffic. Opened in 1884, it closed in 1955, although freight was handled until 1963.

35. Reached from Station Road, these are the offices and booking hall of **Cross Gates** station, c.1905, with the ramp leading to the westbound platform. The original station, dating from c.1834, was modified c.1902. This card and that on the front cover were produced by Parkinson & Roy, Kelsall Street, Leeds.

36. In 1876, the NER opened a branch from Cross Gates to Wetherby. It became an alternative route for Newcastle-Liverpool expresses. Attractive **Bardsey** station, with its typical NER 'villa type' structure with house, was one of several stations serving local communities. This c.1905 view, by J. Hodgson of Cleckheaton, shows milk churns awaiting collection. The branch closed in 1964.

37. Barbed wire came between photographer and subject on this panorama of **Collingham Bridge** station, on the Cross Gates-Wetherby branch. Sidings on the right include a loading dock with round timber. Grain, potatoes and livestock were handled. The card, by William Bramley, Cross Gates, was posted from Collingham to London in 1913.

38. The **Micklefield** station shown here, c.1920, was built c.1880. It replaced the original station opened in 1834 when the Leeds & Selby Railway was constructed. Staggered platforms are clearly visible; also worker's housing on the right. With sidings nearby, Micklefield handled limestone from local quarries. A colliery, half a mile west at Peckfield, also generated business.

39. Kippax station was on the Garforth-Castleford branch which opened in 1878 to serve a colliery area. On this Edwardian vista, the 'villa type' station building and water tower are surrounded by extensive gardens, which had just won a first prize. The station was closed to passengers in 1951 and goods in 1963. Card published by A. & G. Taylor, Bradford.

40. A lively scene at the NER's **Castleford** station, c.1905. It opened in 1871; its predecessor of 1840 was situated further east. The name became Castleford Central in 1952 to avoid confusion with Castleford Cutsyke (former L&Y) station. Over the years the now run-down station has handled chemicals, bricks and glass products.

41. Originally opened in 1840, **Wakefield Kirkgate** station was completely rebuilt in 1857 for the L&Y and GNR. Here, staff and children pose in front of part of the classical facade, c.1908. Extensive goods facilities and a large engine shed were located nearby. Today, the station lives in the shadow of former glory. Wakefield photographers C. & J. Hall produced the card.

42. East from Wakefield, the L&Y ran to Pontefract Tanshelf and Monkhill stations. First stop was **Crofton** station, captured here c.1905. Coal traffic kept the line active, but the station, which opened in 1853, was closed to passengers in 1931, partly because a WR&G counterpart was more conveniently sited.

43. *"The dust and litter from station platforms must not be swept on to the line, but removed to the ashpit"* - L&Y instruction, 1912. It appears that the directive was heeded at **Crigglestone** station on the Barnsey line from Wakefield. The card was produced by H.M. Wilson, Wakefield, c.1912.

44. Before distinctive station styles evolved, station buildings sometimes resembled houses. **Haigh** station, above, and Crigglestone, top, are examples. Each station was opened in 1850 and closed in 1965. The milk churns and coal wagons are symbolic of the area's rural and mining connections. This card was produced by H. Bedford, Clayton West, c.1922.

45. Passengers alighting at **Horbury & Ossett** station (situated at Horbury Bridge) faced a 2.5 mile road journey to Ossett. The station, on the first trans-Pennine route, was named Horbury when opened in 1840. The island platform and six sets of 'through' tracks are depicted here, c.1904. The station was abandoned in 1970.

46. The L&Y built **Dewsbury Market Place** station at the end of a short branch which left its trans-Pennine line near Thornhill. Opened in 1867 and closed in 1930, the station is shown c.1925, with stone side walls supporting an iron and glass roof. Adjacent goods sheds handled mungo and shoddy.

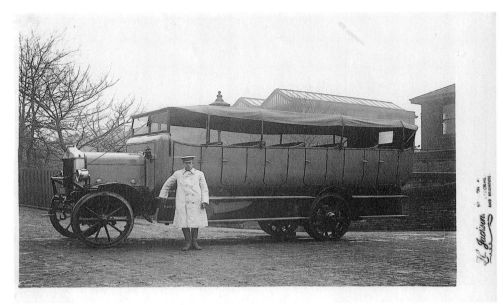

47. The L&Y's Spen Valley line opened in 1848. Its **Cleckheaton** station was rebuilt with an island platform in the 1880s. Here, a solid-tyred charabanc on an AEC chassis, and a 12mph speed restriction, is parked on the station approach in Tofts Road, c.1920. The line was closed to passengers in 1965.

COPYRIGHT
HX.A. 227

BEACON HILL FROM THE STATION, HALIFAX

LILYWHITE LTD.
BRIGHOUSE.

48. Halifax station approach in LMS days. Of the town's three stations, only this remains open. It was formerly shared by the L&Y and GNR. The card, by Lilywhite of Brighouse, was posted in 1938. The wealth of detail includes taxis, tramlines and an ingeniously placed advert for Webster's Green Label.

HIPPERHOLME STATION.

49. Hipperholme station was on the Halifax to Low Moor (and Bradford) line of the L&Y. The station, viewed here c.1920, was large for the area served, although the nearby Sunny Vale Gardens and several local industries helped to generate its business. Opened in 1850, the station closed to passengers in 1953 and goods in 1966.

50. In 1849, the L&Y opened a line from Todmorden to Burnley, which gave access to Blackburn and Blackpool. Its **Cornholme** station was built in 1878. Set against a background of Pennine hills and mill chimneys, the two simple platforms look neatly held together by the footbridge in this c.1903 picture. The station was closed in 1938 but the line remains open.

51. Built in 1847-8 for the L&Y and Huddersfield & Manchester Railway (later L&NW), **Huddersfield** station remains architecturally unrivalled by any other large station in the area. The central building, with pedimented portico and Corinthian columns, originally served as the hotel. The card, by Valentine of Dundee, shows a 'torpedo' charabanc destined for Southport.

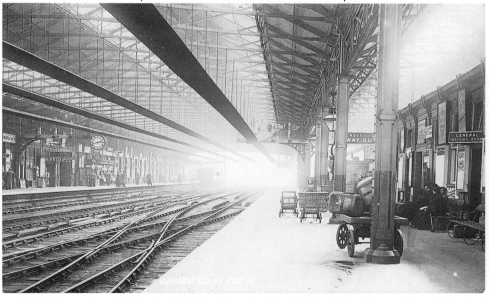

52. This card, published c.1905 by Bamforth of Holmfirth, shows the original platform of **Huddersfield** station on the left. Part of the island platform, added in 1886, is on the right. Of particular interest are the track and roof details, plus static and movable platform paraphernalia.

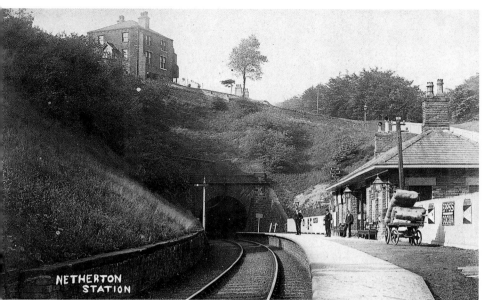

53. Netherton station was on the L&Y branch from Huddersfield to Meltham. The 1905 postcard shows a stone building (with booking office, waiting rooms and conveniences) which was typical of other stations on this largely single-track line. Meltham provided much of the industrial business. Opening in 1868, the branch closed to passengers in 1949 and freight in 1965.

54. The GCR's slight incursion into the region included **Ryhill** station, which opened in 1882. The card was posted from there to Painthorpe, 4.5 miles away, in 1905. The simple timber building seems dominated by the angular metal footbridge. Observe the small awning above the booking hall door. Passenger services ceased in 1930; goods in 1961.

55. In 1867, the Kirkburton branch of the L&NW was opened from the company's Huddersfield-Leeds line at Deighton. The 1904 photograph shows the branch's **Kirkheaton** station. The mainly wooden building has an overhanging roof and small additional awning. The branch lost its passenger service in 1930; goods facilities existed at Kirkburton until 1965.

56. The L&NW's last station on the Yorkshire side, before the line plunged into Standedge tunnel, was **Marsden**. Opening in 1865 to serve a textile area, the station is now much rationalised. The Edwardian gentlemen, including the tweedy character on the right, look set for an outing.

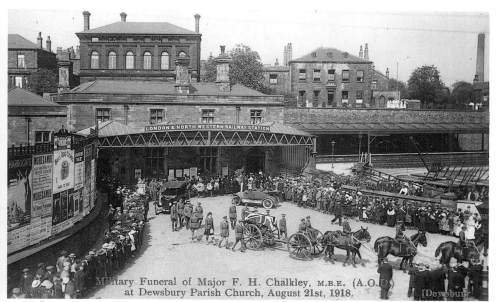

Military Funeral of Major F. H. Chalkley, M.B.E. (A.O.D.) at Dewsbury Parish Church, August 21st, 1918. [Dewsbury

57. Dewsbury Wellington Road, the town's only surviving station, was opened in 1848. This card, by Fred Hartley, photographer, Dewsbury, shows the funeral of Major F.H. Chalkley on 21st August 1918. His body was brought by rail from Llandudno (where he had been convalescing) and paraded through Dewsbury on a gun carriage, before interment in the churchyard.

58. Morley Low station during Morley Feast, c.1903. On a day excursion to Blackpool, people board the non-corridor coaches, a problem for those wishing to 'spend a penny'. This L&NW station, which opened in 1848, is still in use. Morley Top station (GNR) closed in 1961.

59. With textile business in mind, the L&NW opened a rival line through the Spen Valley in 1900 and duplicated the L&Y's Cleckheaton, Liversedge and Heckmondwike stations. The timber buildings at the L&NW's **Heckmondwike** station, shown here c.1905, include the stationmaster's office, waiting rooms and toilets. The line was closed to passengers in 1953.

60. The H&B infiltrated the southeastern tip of the region. Its **Hemsworth & South Kirkby** station was opened in 1891. It closed to passengers in 1932 and goods in 1940. The card, by local photographer Wales, was posted in 1905. It shows gardens, the booking office and a notice board advertising travel to London and Hull.

61. After some wrangling, the GNR and Manchester, Sheffield & Lincolnshire (later GCR) companies acquired the newly promoted West Riding & Grimsby Railway, with effect from opening day, 1st February 1866. This gave the GNR a Wakefield-Doncaster link. **Sandal**, the first station south of Wakefield, is shown c.1913 on a card by H.M. Wilson. Closed in 1957, the station was reopened as Sandal & Agbrigg in 1987.

62. The WR&G built four attractive and similar stations, epitomized here by **South Elmsall**, c.1912. The main station building, in rock-faced stone, has a chapel-cum-cottage style of architecture, with hipped roofs and spire. Bereft of its appealing buildings, the station remains open.

63. Pictured c.1905 on a card by local photographer Wales, the main building at **Hemsworth** station is the same style as that at South Elmsall, but in brick. Note the vending machines and drinking fountain. With sidings at most of its stations and lines to pits, the WR&G reaped benefits from the colliery and agricultural area which it served.

S 4376   BAGHILL STATION, PONTEFRACT.

64. A joint line, known as the Swinton & Knottingley Railway, was constructed by the NER and MR. One of its stations, **Pontefract Baghill**, dating from 1879, is pictured c.1910 on a W.H. Smith 'Kingsway' series postcard. The platform buildings show features associated with both companies. Today, infrequent passenger trains use the station.